"The Four Seasons"
Op. 8, Nos. 1–4
Edited by Eleanor Selfridge-Field

Antonio Vivaldi

DOVER PUBLICATIONS, INC.
Mineola, New York

Bibliographical Note

This Dover edition, first published in 1999, reprints a portion of the edition first published in 1995 by Dover Publications, Inc., New York, under the title *"The Four Seasons" and Other Violin Concertos in Full Score / Opus 8, Complete / Antonio Vivaldi / Edited by Eleanor Selfridge-Field*—a publication made possible with the support and assistance of Edmund Correia Jr. and The Center for Computer Assisted Research in the Humanities, California.

The original frontmatter has been edited to reflect the contents of the present edition. The sonnet texts have been reproduced as they appeared in the original publication.

· *International Standard Book Number: 0–486–40644-X*

Manufactured in the United States of America
Dover Publications, Inc., 31 East 2nd Street, Mineola, N.Y. 11501

CONTENTS

Il Cimento dell'armonia e dell'inventione
(The Contest of Harmony and Invention)

Concertos for Violin, Strings and Continuo
(Opus 8 / early 1720s)

INTRODUCTION

Vivaldi's violin concertos "The Four Seasons" constitute one of the best known and best loved collections of string repertory in our time. Their programmatic nature makes them easily accessible to a general audience. The bird calls in "Spring," the swarms of wasps in "Summer," the hunters' horns in "Autumn," or the narrator's chattering teeth in "Winter" are readily discernible. That these images are so easily communicated by sound alone is, in our visually oriented age, a consoling testimony to the evocative power of aural art.

Less well known are the eight concertos that together with "The Four Seasons" made up Op. 8, all of which appear to have been composed in the early 1720s. The full collection, *Il Cimento dell'armonia e dell'inventione* ("The Contest of Harmony and Invention"), was issued by the publisher Michel-Charles Le Cène in Amsterdam in 1725. It was dedicated by Vivaldi to the Bohemian Count Wenceslas, Count of Morzin, an advisor to the Austrian Emperor Charles VI.

Vivaldi was engaged as a string teacher in the Venetian Ospedale (orphanage-conservatory) of the Pietà in 1703. Although his first published opus (1705) contained chamber sonatas, Vivaldi soon became involved in the composition of string works—both sonatas and concertos—better suited to the needs of a sacred institution. His reputation as a virtuoso spread rapidly. It attracted daughters of the nobility to seek places in the Pietà's music program, which had originally been designed for foundling girls, and it created great demand abroad for Vivaldi's compositions.

Vivaldi's skills as a composer were enhanced by other callings. In 1713, when his superior Francesco Gasparini moved to Rome, Vivaldi was called upon to compose sacred vocal music for the Pietà. In the same year he became active as a composer of operas. Vivaldi left Venice to direct music for Prince Philip of Hesse-Darmstadt at his court in Mantua at the start of 1718 and stayed for three years.

Vivaldi's theatrical activities had more to do with his instrumental music than might be supposed. His violin solos at intermissions became legendary. According to the account of a German nobleman, J. Fr. A. von Uffenbach, who in 1715 attended three performances of one of Vivaldi's operas, the composer "made his fingers jump to the point where there was only a hair's breadth between them and the bridge. He did this while playing imitative passages on all four strings at incredible speed." In 1724 Vivaldi went to Rome for the production of his opera *Giustino*, which offered a proving ground for the opening theme of "Spring." A simpler version of this theme was used in the sinfonia of Act I. It accompanied the descent of the goddess Fortuna, on her wheel, to the stage.

Vivaldi explained his reasons for publishing these works in the following way in his dedication of Op. 8:

> Thinking to myself about the long course of years in which I have had the honor of serving Your Highness in the capacity of Master of Music in Italy, I am embarrassed to realize that I have never offered a token of the profound veneration in which I hold you. In consequence I have resolved to print the present volume as a token of my humility at your feet. If among these few, weak concertos you find "The Four Seasons," for so long regarded with indulgence [*compatite*] by the Generous Goodness of Your Highness, I entreat you not to marvel [at my folly], but [rather] to believe that I have thought them worthy of publication because, in fact, they are more substantial [than those you know] insofar as they are accompanied by their sonnets, which contain an absolutely clear declaration of all the things which are depicted in these works. This, I believe, gives them the status of new works. . . . The intelligence that Your Highness possesses in music and the valor of your most virtuous orchestra enable me always to feel confident that my impoverished deeds, in your esteemed hands, will enjoy a greater ascendancy than they merit. . . .

This commentary (the obsequious tone is characteristic of dedications to noble patrons) is unusually informative. It tells us that the works had indeed been circulated, but without their "demonstrative" sonnets, for a number of years. It is evident, both from the commentary and from the music, that they had been polished over a substantial period of time.

The idea of cycles, both natural and man-made, was in vogue at the time among painters, poets, sculptors and philosophers. Bach's *Well-Tempered Clavier*, illustrating the cycle of tonalities, appeared just three years before the publication of Vivaldi's Op. 8. Earlier musical treatments of the seasons included Lully's ballet *Les Saisons* (1661) and an operetta, *Die Vier Jahrszeiten* ("The Four Seasons"), given in Dresden in August 1719 for the wedding of Friedrich August II to Maria Josepha.

Vivaldi does not say who wrote the sonnets on which his works were based. Their texts, which are printed with new translations on pp. xii and xiii of this edition, are presented in tables that serve three purposes. They show the letter designations that Vivaldi used in linking each section of poetry with the music. They show the divergent rhyme schemes employed. Finally, they show how the segmentation of each sonnet into three musical movements was different.

In relation to the popularity of "The Four Seasons," the scarcity of editions reflecting scholarly discoveries of recent years is surprising. The important work of cataloguing manuscript sources of Vivaldi's music, begun in the 1960s and continuing to the present day by Peter Ryom (RV stands for *Ryom Verzeichnis*), has brought to light handwritten examples for all but two of the concertos—Nos. 6 and 12—in Op. 8. However, for only six of the works (5, 7–11) are there manuscript sources predating the print. Collectively, these sources demonstrate that Vivaldi was quick to change his mind, especially about the solo passages in his concertos. There are numerous discrepancies, and many small differences in accompaniment style, continuo figuration and bowing are found from source to source.

This new edition, while being based mainly on the 1725 print, gives Vivaldi's (or his Saxon pupil Pisendel's) bowings and figurations, where available, in the *Violino Principale*. It restores continuo figuration changed in the print to what is found in autograph sources and adds numerous figures to enable today's performers to provide a satisfactory realization. It offers needed corrections to pitches and rhythms. It supplies dynamics markings and ornament indications given erratically in the print. Lastly, it retrieves from Vivaldi's autographs variant readings not available in other editions.

Dr. Eleanor Selfridge-Field

"The Four Seasons"
SONNET TEXTS

"The Four Seasons": Sonnet Texts

1. *La Primavera* ("Spring")

Mvt.	Sec.	Rhyme	Italian text	English translation
I	A	a	Giunt' è la primavera e festosetti	Spring has come, and birds greet it
	B	b	La salutan gl'augei con lieto canto;	Festively with a cheerful song;
	C	a	E i fonti allo spirar de' zeffiretti	And with the breath of gentle breezes
		b	Con dolce mormorio scorrono intanto.	Springs trickle with a sweet murmur.
	D	b	Vengon' coprendo l'aer di nero amanto,	Lightning and thunder, elected to announce it,
		a	E lampi e tuoni ad annuntiarla eletti.	Come and cover the air with a black cloak.
	E	a	Indi tacendo questi, gl'augelletti	Once they are quiet, the birds
		b	Toman' di nuovo al lor canoro incanto.	Return to their enchanting song.
II	F	c	E quindi sul fiorito ameno prato	Then on the pleasant, flowered meadow
		d	Al caro mormorio di fronde e piante.	A goatherd, with his faithful dog at his side,
		c	Dorme 'l caprar col fido can' al lato.	Sleeps to the sweet murmur of fronds and plants.
III	G	d	Di pastoral zampogna al suon festante	To the festive sound of a rustic bagpipe
		c	Danzan' ninfe e pastori nel tetto amato	Nymphs and shepherds dance under the beloved canopy
		d	Di primavera all'apparir brillante.	At the brilliant appearance of spring.

2. *L'Estate* ("Summer")

I	A	a	Sotto dura staggion' dal sole accesa	Under the harsh season ignited by the sun
		b	Langue l'huom, langue 'l gregge, ed arde il pino;	Man and flock languish, and the pine burns;
	B	a	Scioglie il cucco la voce, e tosto intesa	The cuckoo offers his voice, and, soon heard,
	C	b	Canta la tortorella e 'l gardelino.	The young turtledove and goldfinch sing.
	D	a	Zeffiro dolce spira, ma contesa	Zephyr[1] blows gently, but suddenly
		b	Muove Borea improviso al suo vicino;	Boreas[2] offers opposition to his neighbor;
	E	a	E piange il pastorel, perche sospesa	And the shepherd weeps, because he fears
		b	Teme fiera borasca, e 'l suo destino.	A severe storm in the offing—and his destiny.
II	F	c	Toglie alle membra lasse il suo riposo	The repose of his tired limbs is disturbed
		d	Il timore de' lampi, e tuoni fieri,	By the fear of lightning and fiery thunder,
		c	E de mosche e mossoni il stuol furioso!	And by a furious swarm of flies and wasps.
III	G	d	Ah, che pur troppo i suoi timor' son veri.	Unfortunately, his fears are justified.
		c	Tuona e fulmina il Ciel, e grandinoso	The sky thunders and fulminates, and hail
		d	Tronca il capo alle spiche e a' grani alteri.	Flattens ears of corn and majestic grains.

---

[1] The West Wind.

[2] The North Wind.

3. *L'Autunno* ("Autumn")

Mvt.	Sec.	Rhyme	Italian text	English translation
I	A	a	Celebra il vilanel con balli e canti	The peasant celebrates the blissful pleasure
		b	Del felice raccolto il bel piacere,	Of a happy harvest with dances and songs,
	B	a	E del liquor di Bacco accesi tanti	And, glowing with the liquor of Bacchus,
	C	b	Finiscono col sonno il lor godere.	Many complete their enjoyment with sleep.
II	D	a	Fa ch'ogn'uno tralasci e balli e canti,	The air, tempered by pleasure, makes
		b	L'aria che temperata dà piacere.	Everyone give up dances and songs.
		a	È la staggion ch'invita tanti e tanti	It is the season that invites so many
		b	D'un dolcissimo sonno al bel godere.	To the great enjoyment of a sweet sleep.
III	E	c	I cacciator' alla nov'alba a caccia	At dawn the hunters are off to the hunt
		d	Con corni, schioppi, e canni escono fuore.	With horns, rifles, and dogs.
	F	c	Fugge la belva, e seguono la traccia.	The wild beast flees, and they follow its trail.
	G	d	Già sbigottita, e lassa al gran rumore	Frightened already, and fatigued by the noise
		c	De' schioppi e canni, ferita, minaccia	Of rifles and dogs, wounded, it threatens
	H	d	Languida di fuggir, ma oppressa, muore.	Languidly to flee, but, overcome, it dies.

4. *L'Inverno* ("Winter")

I	A	a	Aggiacciato tremar tra nevi algenti	To tremble from cold in the icy snow,
	B	b	Al severo spirar d'orrido vento,	In the harsh breath of a horrid wind;
	C	b	Correr battendo i piedi ogni momento;	To run, stamping our feet every moment,
	D	a	E pel soverchio gel batter i denti;	Our teeth chattering in the extreme cold.
II	E	a	Passar al fuoco i dì quieti e contenti	Before the fire to pass peaceful,
		b	Mentre la pioggia fuor bagna ben cento.	Contented days while the rain outside pours down.
III	F	b	Caminar sopra 'l giaccio, e a passo lento,	To walk on the ice and, at a slow pace,
	G	a	Per timor di cader, girsene intenti.	(For fear of falling), move carefully.
	H	c	Gir³ forte, sdruzziolar, cader a terra,	To make a bold turn, slip, fall down.
	I	d	Di nuovo ir sopra 'l giaccio e correr forte	To go on the ice once more and run hard
	L	c	Sinch' il giaccio si rompe e si disserra;	Until the ice cracks and breaks up.
	M	d	Sentir uscir dalle ferrate porte	To hear the Sirocco, Boreas, and all
	N	c	Sirocco, Borea, e tutti i venti in guerra.	The winds at war leave their iron gates:
		d	Quest'è 'l verno, ma tal che gioia apporte.	This is winter, but, even so, what joy it brings!

---

³ "Andare," which does not fit the poetic meter, is found in some partbooks.

"The Four Seasons"

Concerto No. 1 in E Major

La Primavera ("Spring")

I.

1

15

19
e festosetti

22
(B) *La salutan gl'augei con lieto canto;*

[Trickling of the springs]
Scorrono i fonti
(C) *E i fonti allo spirar de' zeffiretti   Con dolce mormorio scorrono intanto.*

[Thunder]
Tuoni
(D) *Vengon' coprendo l'aer di nero amanto, E lampi e tuoni ad*

annuntiarla eletti.

[Song of the birds]
Canto degl'uccelli
(E) *Indi tacendo questi, gl'augelletti*

Tornan' di nuovo al lor canoro incant

Tasto solo

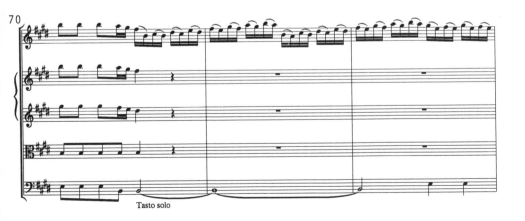

Tasto solo

II.

III.

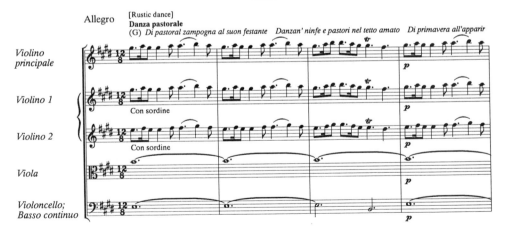

Tasto solo

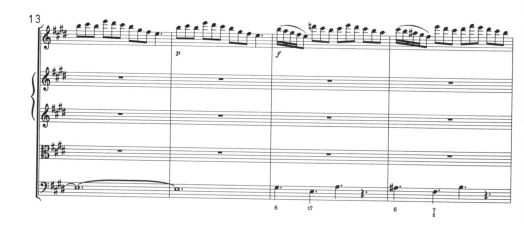

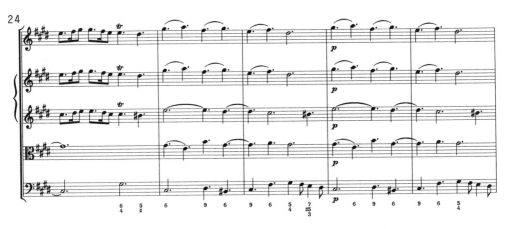

Tasto solo

Tasto solo

6

Tasto solo

Concerto No. 2 in G Minor
L'Estate ("Summer")
I.

Allegro non molto

Languidezza per il caldo [Exhausted by the heat]
(A) *Sotto dura staggion' dal sole accesa Langue l'huom, langue 'l gregge,*

(Op. 8, No. 2 / RV 315)

ed arde il pino;

Allegro

Il cucco [The cuckoo]
(B) *Scioglie il cucco la voce, e tosto intesa*

Tutto sopra il canto

19

Sopra il cantino

La tortorella

[The turtledove]

La tortorella

(C) *Canta la tortorella e 'l gardelino.*

Tasto solo

Allegro non molto

[The goldfinch]
Il gardellino

[Gentle breezes]
Zeffiretti dolci
(D) *Zeffiro dolce spira,*

Vento Borea [The North Wind]
ma contesa   Muove Borea improviso al suo vicino;

104

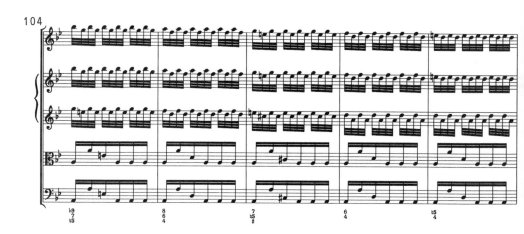

[The tears of the village boy]
Il pianto del villanello
(E) *E piange il pastorel, perchè sospesa*

109

Teme fiera borasca, e 'l suo destino.

119

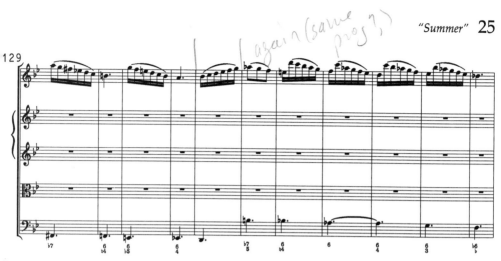

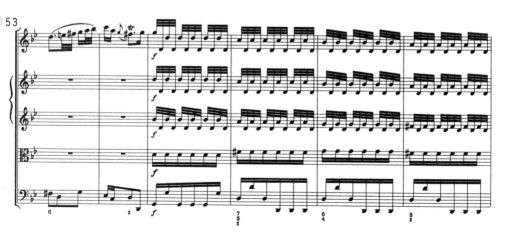

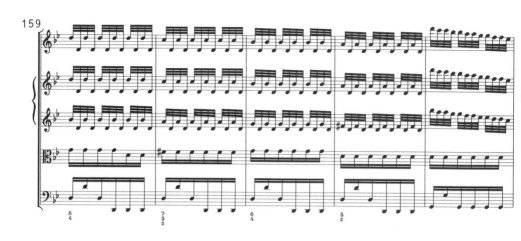

II.

III.

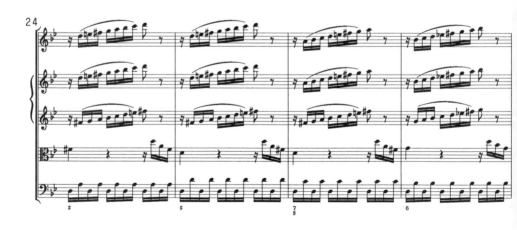

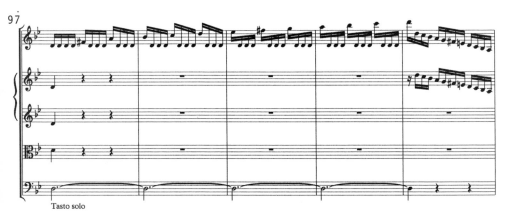

Concerto No. 3 in F Major
L'Autunno ("Autumn")
I.

double steps!

25

29

[The drunkard]
L'Ubriaco
(B) *E del liquor di*

33

Bacco accesi tanti

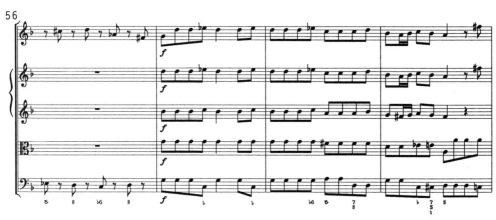

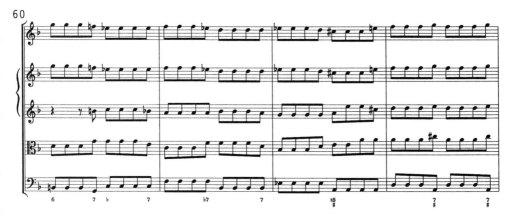

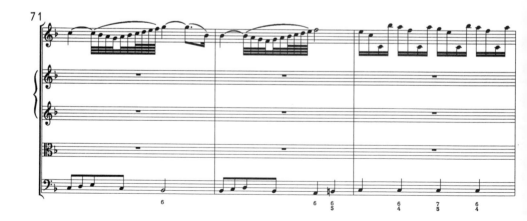

84

Larghetto [The dozing
L'Ubriaco che dorme drunkard]
(C) *Finiscono col sonno il lor godere.*

87

91

Allegro assai

II.

Ubriachi dormenti [Dozing drunkards]
(D) *Fa ch'ogn'uno tralasci e balli e canti, L'aria che temperata dà piacere.*

Adagio molto

Violino principale
Violino 1
Violino 2
Viola
Violoncello; Basso continuo

Con sordini
Con sordini
Con sordini
Il cembalo arpeggio

13 *È la staggion ch'invita tanti e tanti D'un dolcissimo sonno al bel godere.*

sempre **p**

28

p *più* **p** **pp**

III.

La fiera che fugge [The wild beast flees]
(F) *Fugge la belva, e seguono la traccia.*

(G) *Già sbigottita, e lassa al gran rumore*   *De' schioppi e canni, ferita, minaccia*

La fiera, fuggendo, muore [The beast, fleeing, dies]
(H) *Languida di fuggir, ma oppressa, muore.*

Tasto solo

Concerto No. 4 in F Minor

L'Inverno ("Winter")

I.

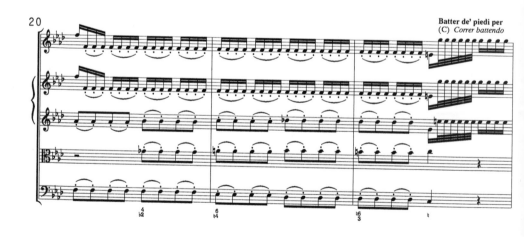

il freddo [To stamp one's feet from the cold]
i piedi ogni momento;

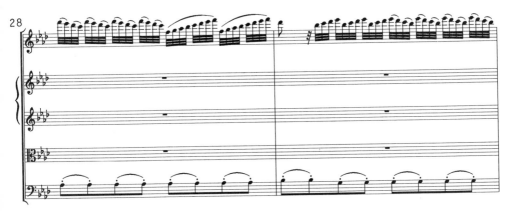

Venti [Winds]

double steps

Batter li denti [Chattering of teeth]
(D) *E pel soverchio gel batter i denti;*

II.

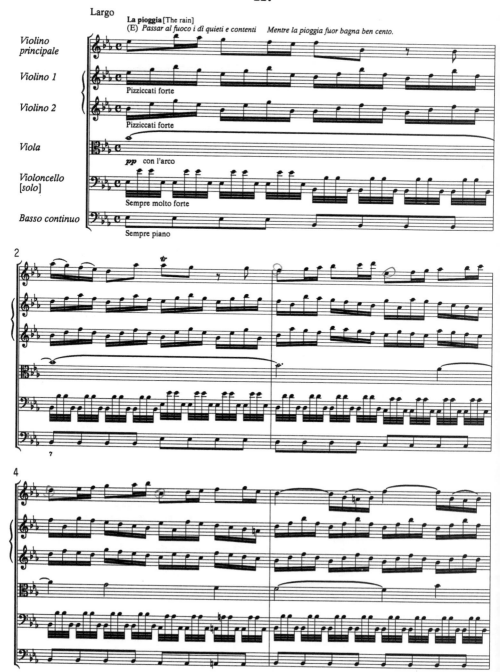

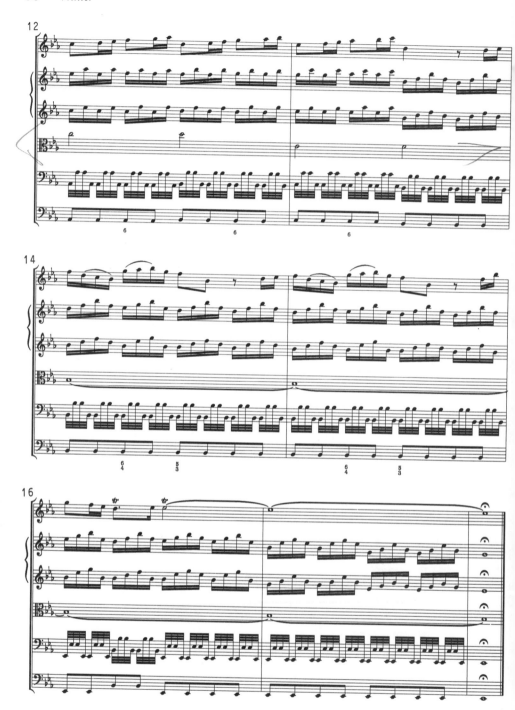

III.

Allegro

(F) *Caminar sopra 'l giaccio,*

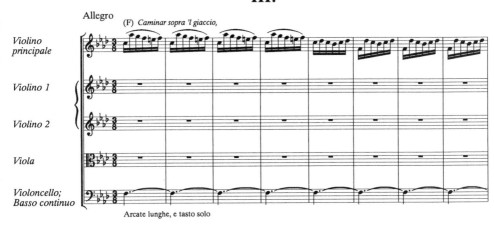

Violino principale

Violino 1

Violino 2

Viola

Violoncello; Basso continuo

Arcate lunghe, e tasto solo

9

[Walking slowly and fearfully]
Caminar piano e con timore

e a passo lento, (G) *Per timor di cader, girsene intenti.*

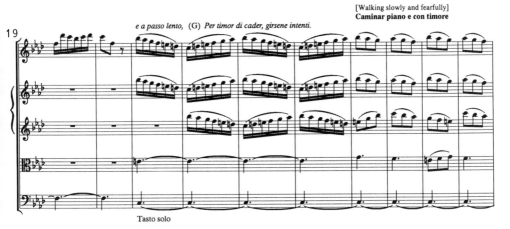

19

Tasto solo

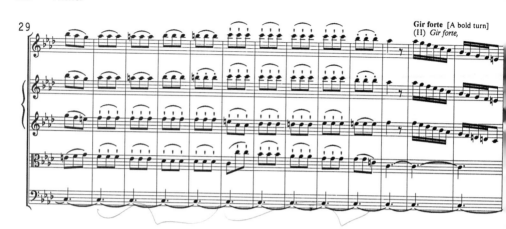

Tasto solo

Tasto solo

Breakensice

(L) *Sinch' il giaccio si rompe e si disserra;*

Lento
Il vento Sirocco [Sirocco (the hot desert wind)]
(M) *Sentir uscir dalle ferrate porte*

[Boreas (the cold North Wind)]
Il vento Borea
(N) *Sirocco, Borea, e tutti*

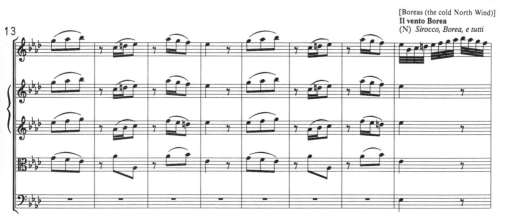

i venti in guerra.

e tutti li venti [and all the winds]

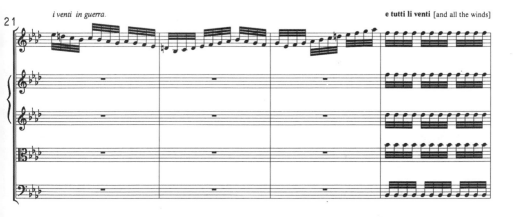

141

145

Quest'è 'l verno, ma tal che gioia

149

apporte.

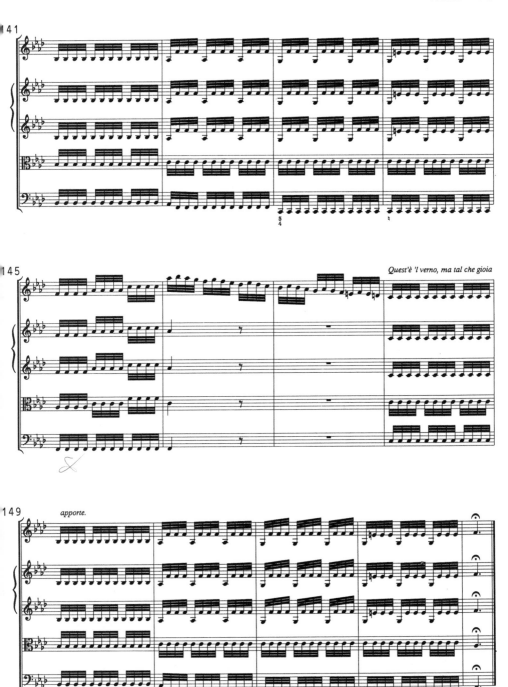

END OF EDITION

DOVER FULL-SIZE
ORCHESTRAL SCORES

**THE SIX BRANDENBURG CONCERTOS AND THE FOUR ORCHES-
TRAL SUITES IN FULL SCORE, Johann Sebastian Bach.** Complete
standard Bach-Gesellschaft editions in large, clear format. Study
score. 273pp. 9 x 12. 23376-6

**COMPLETE CONCERTI FOR SOLO KEYBOARD AND ORCHESTRA
IN FULL SCORE, Johann Sebastian Bach.** Bach's seven complete
concerti for solo keyboard and orchestra in full score from the
authoritative Bach-Gesellschaft edition. 206pp. 9 x 12. 24929-8

**THE THREE VIOLIN CONCERTI IN FULL SCORE, Johann
Sebastian Bach.** Concerto in A Minor, BWV 1041; Concerto in E
Major, BWV 1042; and Concerto for Two Violins in D Minor, BWV
1043. Bach-Gesellschaft edition. 64pp. 9⅜ x 12¼. 25124-1

**GREAT ROMANTIC VIOLIN CONCERTI IN FULL SCORE, Ludwig
van Beethoven, Felix Mendelssohn and Peter Ilyitch Tchaikovsky.**
The Beethoven Op. 61, Mendelssohn, Op. 64, and Tchaikovsky, Op.
35 concertos, reprinted from the Breitkopf & Härtel editions. 224pp.
9 x 12. 24989-1

**SYMPHONIES NOS. 1, 2, 3, AND 4 IN FULL SCORE, Ludwig van
Beethoven.** Republication of H. Litolff edition. 272pp. 9 x 12.
26033-X

**SYMPHONIES NOS. 5, 6 AND 7 IN FULL SCORE, Ludwig van
Beethoven.** Republication of the H. Litolff edition. 272pp. 9 x 12.
26034-8

**SYMPHONIES NOS. 8 AND 9 IN FULL SCORE, Ludwig van
Beethoven.** Republication of the H. Litolff edition. 256pp. 9 x 12.
26035-6

SIX GREAT OVERTURES IN FULL SCORE, Ludwig van Beethoven.
Six staples of the orchestral repertoire from authoritative Breitkopf
& Härtel edition. *Leonore Overtures,* Nos. 1–3; Overtures to
Coriolanus, Egmont, Fidelio. 288pp. 9 x 12. 24789-9

**COMPLETE PIANO CONCERTOS IN FULL SCORE, Ludwig van
Beethoven.** Complete scores of five great Beethoven piano concertos, with all cadenzas as he wrote them, reproduced from authoritative Breitkopf & Härtel edition. New table of contents. 384pp.
9⅜ x 12¼. 24563-2

**THREE ORCHESTRAL WORKS IN FULL SCORE: Academic Festival
Overture, Tragic Overture and Variations on a Theme by Joseph
Haydn, Johannes Brahms.** Reproduced from the authoritative
Breitkopf & Härtel edition, three of Brahms's great orchestral
favorites. Editor's commentary in German and English. 112pp.
9⅜ x 12¼. 24637-X

COMPLETE CONCERTI IN FULL SCORE, Johannes Brahms. Piano Concertos Nos. 1 and 2; Violin Concerto, Op. 77; Concerto for Violin and Cello, Op. 102. Definitive Breitkopf & Härtel edition. 352pp. 9⅜ x 12¼. 24170-X

COMPLETE SYMPHONIES, Johannes Brahms. Full orchestral scores. No. 1 in C Minor, Op. 68; No. 2 in D Major, Op. 73; No. 3 in F Major, Op. 90; and No. 4 in E Minor, Op. 98. Reproduced from definitive Vienna Gesellschaft der Musikfreunde edition. Study score. 344pp. 9 x 12. 23053-8

SYMPHONY NO. 5 IN B-FLAT MAJOR IN FULL SCORE, Anton Bruckner. Featuring strikingly original harmonies, an extended structure, and tonal range, this staple of the orchestral repertoire is a landmark of the Austro-Germanic symphonic tradition. 192pp. 9 x 12. (Available in U.S. only) 41691-7

THE PIANO CONCERTOS IN FULL SCORE, Frédéric Chopin. The authoritative Breitkopf & Härtel full-score edition in one volume of Piano Concertos No. 1 in E Minor and No. 2 in F Minor. 176pp. 9 x 12. 25835-1

COMPLETE CONCERTI GROSSI IN FULL SCORE, Arcangelo Corelli. All 12 concerti in the famous late nineteenth-century edition prepared by violinist Joseph Joachim and musicologist Friedrich Chrysander. 240pp. 8⅜ x 11¼. 25606-5

THREE GREAT ORCHESTRAL WORKS IN FULL SCORE, Claude Debussy. Three favorites by influential modernist: *Prélude à l'Après-midi d'un Faune, Nocturnes,* and *La Mer.* Reprinted from early French editions. 279pp. 9 x 12. 24441-5

SYMPHONY NO. 8 IN G MAJOR, OP. 88, SYMPHONY NO. 9 IN E MINOR, OP. 95 ("NEW WORLD") IN FULL SCORE, Antonín Dvořák. Two celebrated symphonies by the great Czech composer, the Eighth and the immensely popular Ninth, "From the New World," in one volume. 272pp. 9 x 12. 24749-X

CELLO CONCERTO IN E MINOR, OP. 85, IN FULL SCORE, Edward Elgar. A tour de force for any cellist, this frequently performed work is widely regarded as an elegy for a lost world. Melodic and evocative, it exhibits a remarkable scope, ranging from tragic passion to buoyant optimism. Reproduced from an authoritative source. 112pp. 8⅜ x 11. (Not available in Europe or United Kingdom) 41896-0

SYMPHONY IN D MINOR IN FULL SCORE, César Franck. Superb, authoritative edition of Franck's only symphony, an often-performed and recorded masterwork of late French romantic style. 160pp. 9 x 12. 25373-2

HOLBERG SUITE AND OTHER ORCHESTRAL WORKS IN FULL SCORE, Edvard Grieg. Famed title work, five others: Two Elegiac Melodies, Op. 34; Old Norwegian Romances with Variations, Op. 51; Two Melodies, Op. 53; Lyric Pieces from Opp. 54 and 68. Authoritative C. F. Peters editions. 192pp. 9 x 12. 41692-5

COMPLETE CONCERTI GROSSI IN FULL SCORE, George Frideric Handel. Monumental Opus 6 Concerti Grossi, Opus 3 and "Alexander's Feast" Concerti Grossi—19 in all—reproduced from most authoritative edition. 258pp. 9⅜ x 12¼. 24187-4

GREAT ORGAN CONCERTI, OPP. 4 & 7, IN FULL SCORE, George Frideric Handel. 12 organ concerti composed by great Baroque master are reproduced in full score from the *Deutsche Handelgesellschaft* edition. 138pp. 9⅜ x 12¼. 24462-8

WATER MUSIC AND MUSIC FOR THE ROYAL FIREWORKS IN FULL SCORE, George Frideric Handel. Full scores of two of the most popular Baroque orchestral works performed today—reprinted from definitive Deutsche Handelgesellschaft edition. Total of 96pp. 8⅛ x 11. 25070-9

SYMPHONIES 88–92 IN FULL SCORE: The Haydn Society Edition, Joseph Haydn. Full score of symphonies Nos. 88 through 92. Large, readable noteheads, ample margins for fingerings, etc., and extensive Editor's Commentary. 304pp. 9 x 12. (Available in U.S. only) 24445-8

THE PLANETS IN FULL SCORE, Gustav Holst. Spectacular symphonic suite, scored for large orchestral forces and a wordless chorus, embodies the astrological and mystical qualities of various planets. Only full-size score available. 192pp. 9⅜ x 12¼. (Not available in Europe or United Kingdom) 29277-0

THE PIANO CONCERTI IN FULL SCORE, Franz Liszt. Available in one volume: the Piano Concerto No. 1 in E-flat Major and the Piano Concerto No. 2 in A Major—among the most studied, recorded and performed of all works for piano and orchestra. 144pp. 9 x 12. 25221-3

DAS LIED VON DER ERDE IN FULL SCORE, Gustav Mahler. Mahler's masterpiece, a fusion of song and symphony, reprinted from the original 1912 Universal Edition. English translations of song texts. 160pp. 9 x 12. 25657-X

SYMPHONIES NOS. 1 AND 2 IN FULL SCORE, Gustav Mahler. Unabridged, authoritative Austrian editions of Symphony No. 1 in D Major ("Titan") and Symphony No. 2 in C Minor ("Resurrection"). 384pp. 8⅛ x 11. 25473-9

SYMPHONIES NOS. 3 AND 4 IN FULL SCORE, Gustav Mahler. Two brilliantly contrasting masterworks—one scored for a massive ensemble, the other for small orchestra and soloist—reprinted from authoritative Viennese editions. 368pp. 9⅜ x 12¼. 26166-2

SYMPHONY NO. 8 IN FULL SCORE, Gustav Mahler. Superb authoritative edition of massive, complex "Symphony of a Thousand." Scored for orchestra, eight solo voices, double chorus, boys' choir and organ. Reprint of Izdatel'stvo "Muzyka," Moscow, edition. Translation of texts. 272pp. 9⅜ x 12¼. 26022-4

THE FIREBIRD IN FULL SCORE (Original 1910 Version), Igor Stravinsky. Handsome, inexpensive edition of modern masterpiece, renowned for brilliant orchestration and glowing color. Authoritative Russian edition. 176pp. 9⅜ x 12¼. (Available in U.S. only)   25535-2

FIREWORKS AND SONG OF THE NIGHTINGALE IN FULL SCORE, Igor Stravinsky. *Fireworks* is a brilliant early score written in 1908; *Song of the Nightingale* is a symphonic poem for orchestra. 128pp. 9 x 12 . (Available in U.S. only)   41392-6

PETRUSHKA IN FULL SCORE: Original Version, Igor Stravinsky. The definitive full-score edition of Stravinsky's masterful score for the great Ballets Russes 1911 production of *Petrushka.* 160pp. 9⅜ x 12¼. (Available in U.S. only)   25680-4

THE RITE OF SPRING IN FULL SCORE, Igor Stravinsky. A reprint of the original full-score edition of the most famous musical work of the 20th century, created as a ballet score for Diaghilev's Ballets Russes. 176pp. 9⅜ x 12¼. (Available in U.S. only)   25857-2

FOURTH, FIFTH AND SIXTH SYMPHONIES IN FULL SCORE, Peter Ilyitch Tchaikovsky. Complete orchestral scores of Symphony No. 4 in F minor, Op. 36; Symphony No. 5 in E minor, Op. 64; Symphony No. 6 in B minor, "Pathetique," Op. 74. Study score. Breitkopf & Härtel editions. 480pp. 9⅜ x 12¼.   23861-X

NUTCRACKER SUITE IN FULL SCORE, Peter Ilyitch Tchaikovsky. Among the most popular ballet pieces ever created—a complete, inexpensive, high-quality score to study and enjoy. 128pp. 9 x 12.
                                   25379-1

ROMEO AND JULIET OVERTURE AND CAPRICCIO ITALIEN IN FULL SCORE, Peter Ilyitch Tchaikovsky. Two of Russian master's most popular compositions in high quality, inexpensive reproduction. From authoritative Russian edition. 208pp. 8⅜ x 11½.   25217-5

GREAT OVERTURES IN FULL SCORE, Carl Maria von Weber. Overtures to *Oberon, Der Freischutz, Euryanthe* and *Preciosa* reprinted from authoritative Breitkopf & Härtel editions. 112pp. 9 x 12.   25225-6

Paperbound unless otherwise indicated. Available at your book dealer, online at **www.dover publications.com**, or by writing to Dept. 23, Dover Publications, Inc., 31 East 2nd Street, Mineola, NY 11501. For current price information or for free catalogues (please indicate field of interest), write to Dover Publications or log on to **www.doverpublications.com** and see every Dover book in print. Dover publishes more than 500 books each year on science, elementary and advanced mathematics, biology, music, art, literary history, social sciences, and other areas.
Manufactured in the U.S.A.